Piano • Vocal • Guitar

AVRIL LAVIGNE
the best damn thing

ISBN-13: 978-1-4234-3139-8
ISBN-10: 1-4234-3139-1

HAL•LEONARD®
CORPORATION
7777 W. BLUEMOUND RD. P.O. BOX 13819 MILWAUKEE, WI 53213

In Australia Contact:
Hal Leonard Australia Pty. Ltd.
4 Lentara Court
Cheltenham, Victoria, 3192 Australia
Email: ausadmin@halleonard.com

Visit Hal Leonard Online at
www.halleonard.com

GIRLFRIEND

Words and Music by AVRIL LAVIGNE
and LUKASZ GOTTWALD

mine, you're so de - li - cious. I think a - bout you all the time, you're so ad - dic - tive.

Don't you know what I could do to make you feel al - right, ___ al - right, ___ al - right, ___

___ al - right, ___ al - right? ___ Don't pre - tend, I think you know I'm damn pre - cious.

And hell yeah, I'm the moth - er - ****- in' prin - cess. I can tell you like me

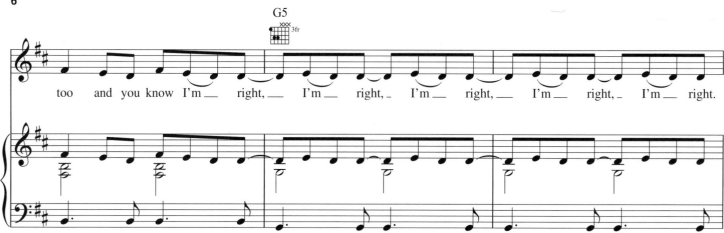

too and you know I'm ___ right, ___ I'm ___ right, ___ I'm ___ right, ___ I'm ___ right, ___ I'm ___ right.

She's like so what-ev - er. You could do

so much bet - ter. I think we should get to-geth - er now ___

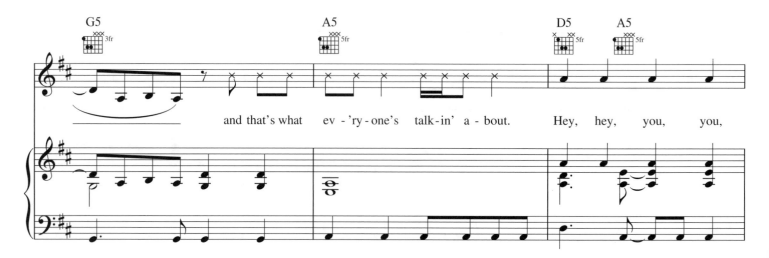

and that's what ev-'ry-one's talk-in' a - bout. Hey, hey, you, you,

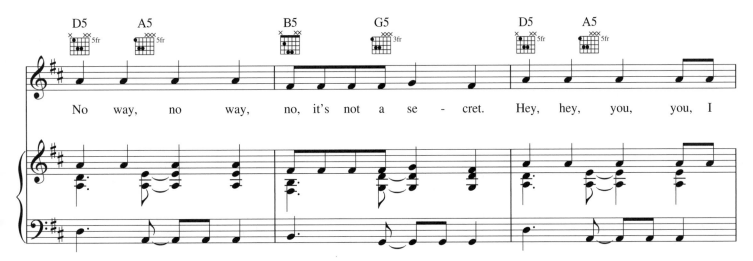

To Coda

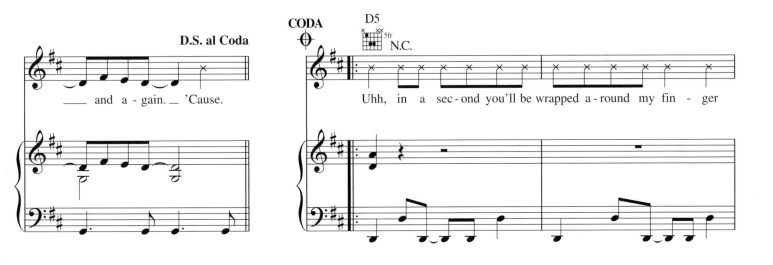

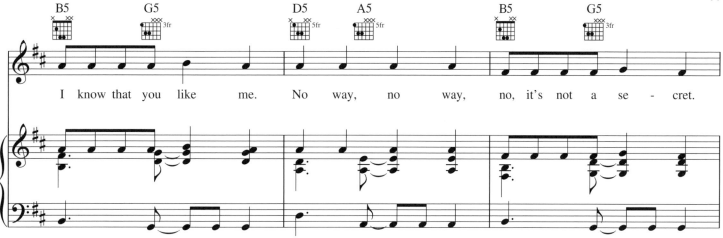

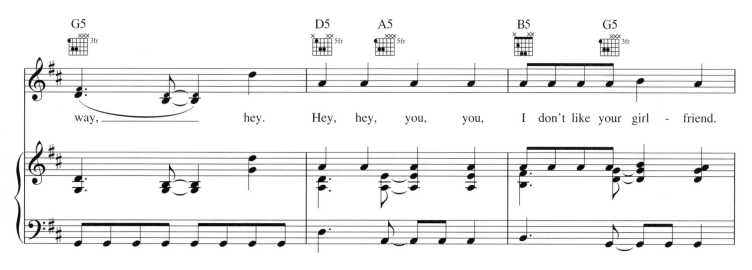

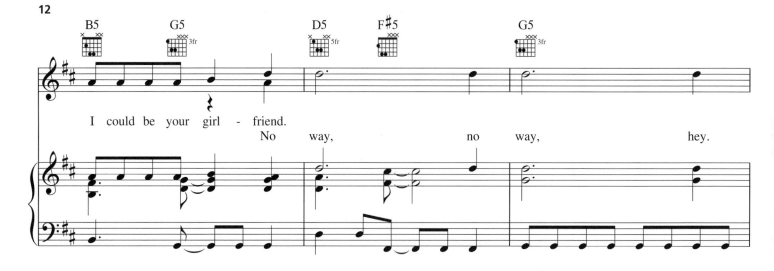

I could be your girl - friend.
No way, no way, hey.

Hey, hey, you, you, I know that you like me. No way, no way,

no, it's not a se - cret. Hey, hey, you, you, I want to be your girl - friend.
No

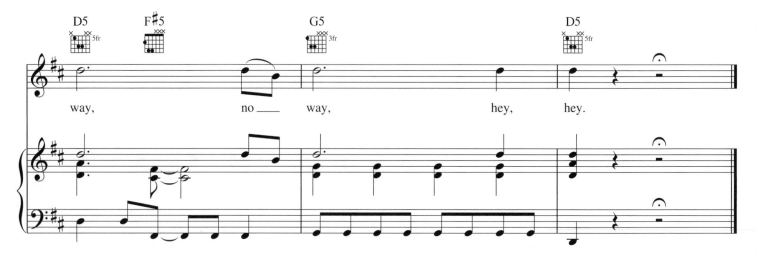

way, no ___ way, hey, hey.

I CAN DO BETTER

Words and Music by AVRIL LAVIGNE
and LUKASZ GOTTWALD

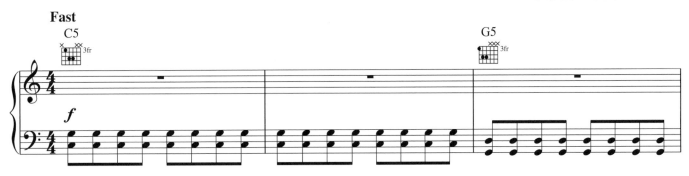

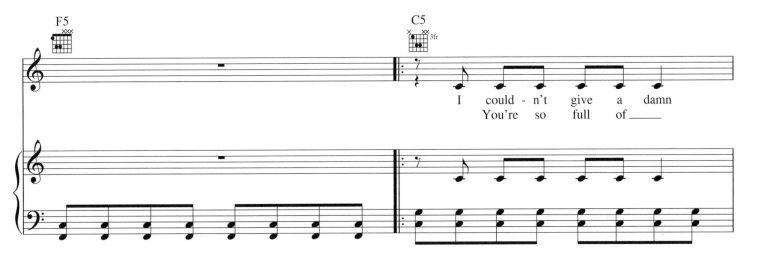

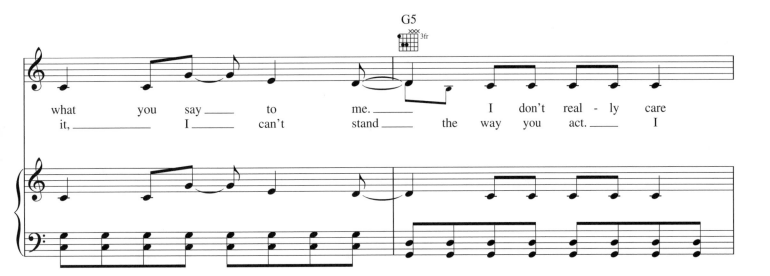

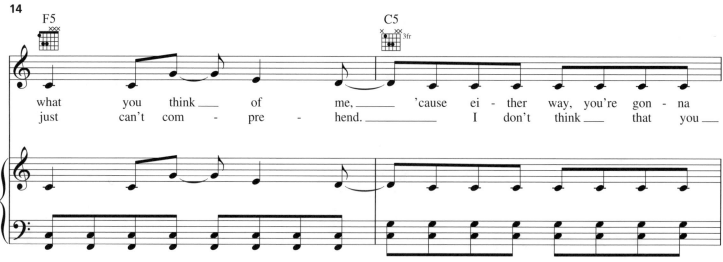

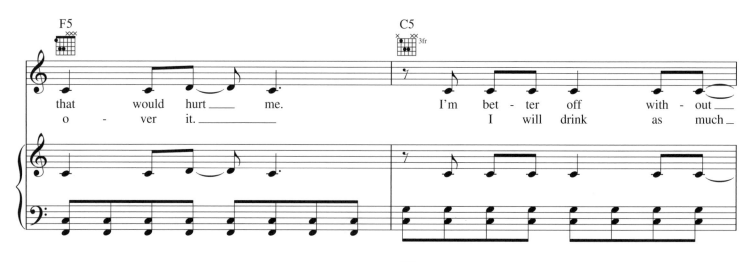

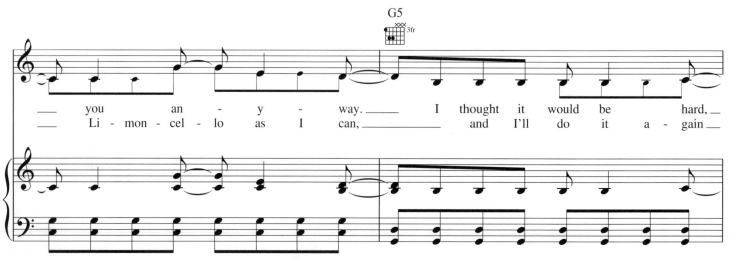

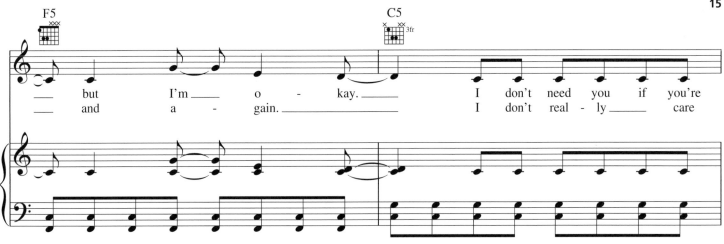

but I'm o - kay. I don't need you if you're
and a - gain. I don't real - ly care

gon - na be that way, 'cause with me it's
what you have to say, 'cause you know, you

all or noth - ing. } I'm sick of { this / your } shit, don't de - ny
know you're noth - ing. }

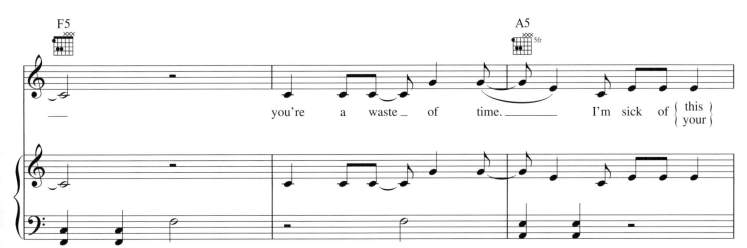

you're a waste of time. I'm sick of { this / your }

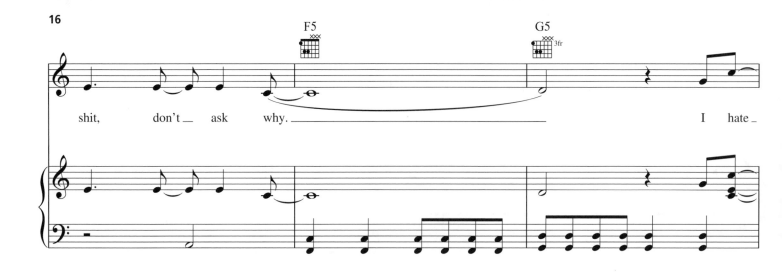

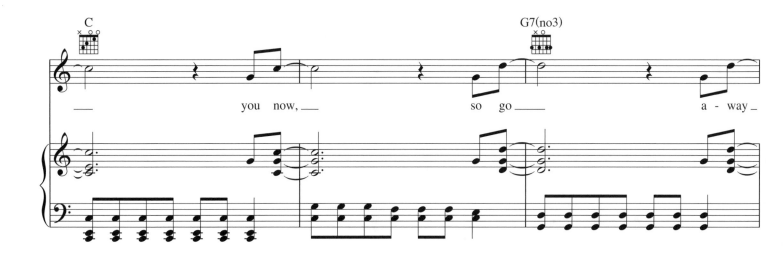

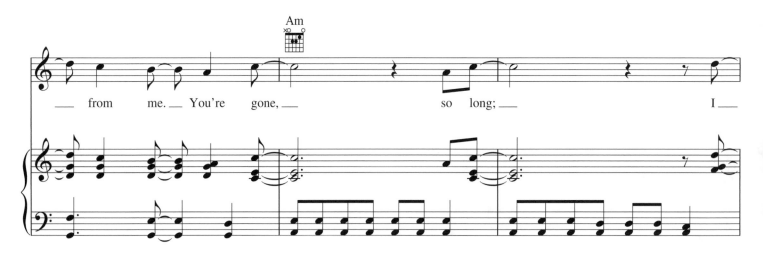

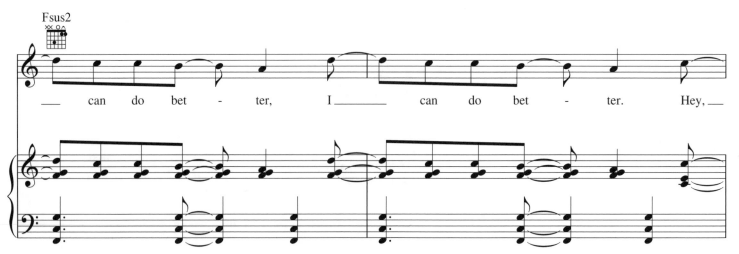

hey you, _____ I found _

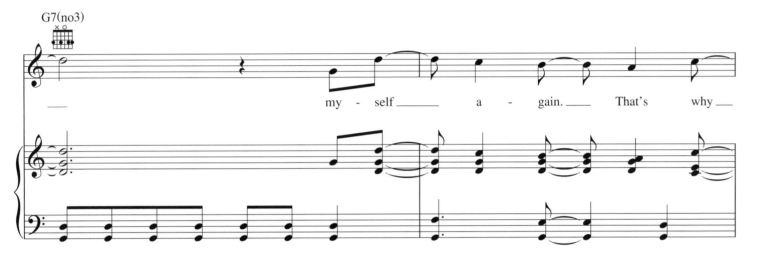

my - self _____ a - gain. _____ That's why _

you're gone. _____ I _____

_ can do bet - ter, I _____ can do bet - ter.

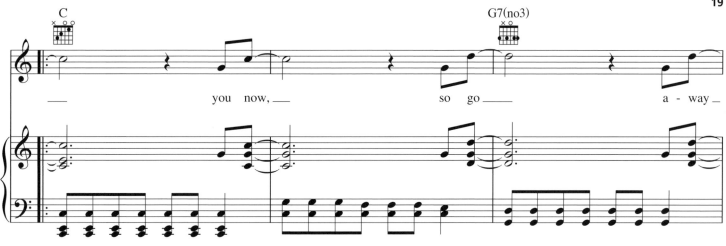

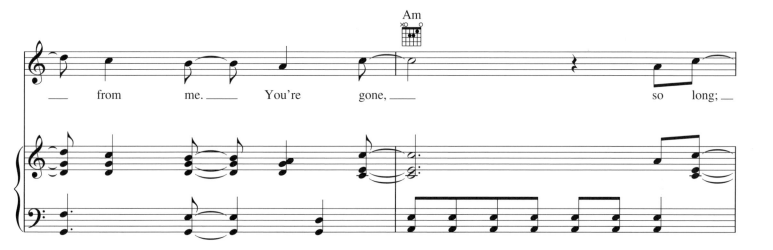

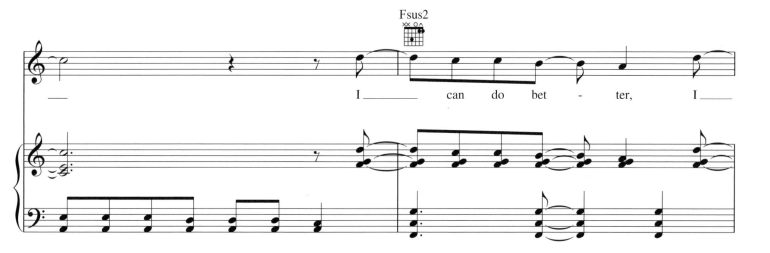

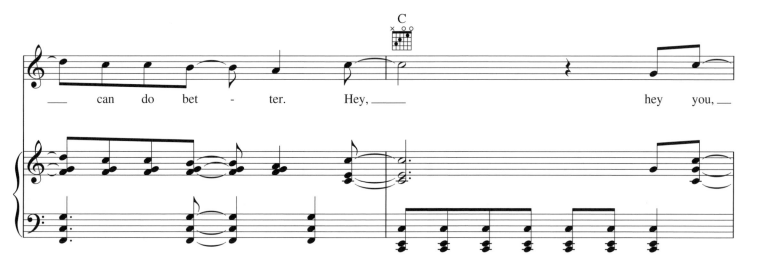

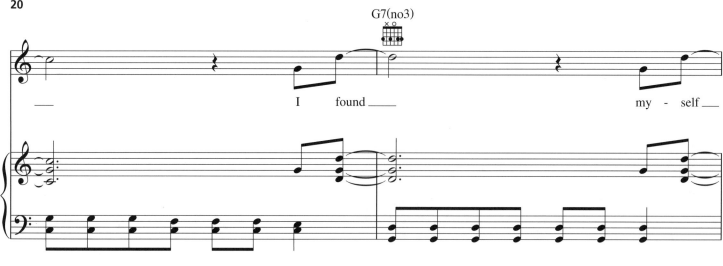

I found ___ my - self ___

___ a - gain. ___ That's why ___ you're gone. ___

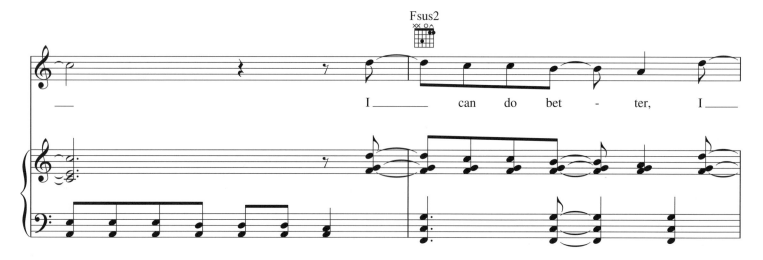

I ___ can do bet - ter, I ___

___ can do bet - ter. I hate ___ can do bet - ter.

RUNAWAY

Words and Music by AVRIL LAVIGNE,
LUKASZ GOTTWALD and KARA DioGUARDI

Moderately fast

Got up on the wrong side of life to-day, yeah. ___ Crashed the

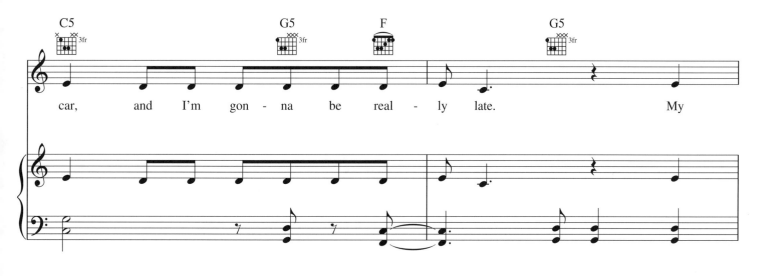

car, and I'm gon-na be real-ly late. My

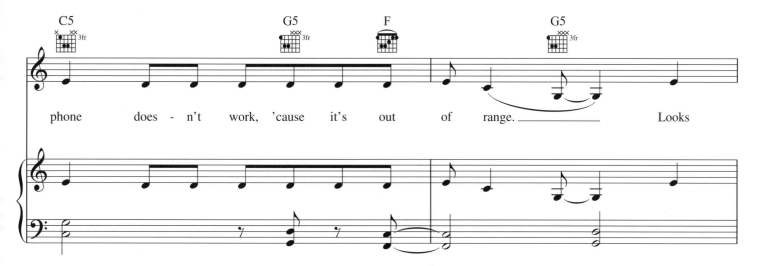

phone does-n't work, 'cause it's out of range. ___ Looks

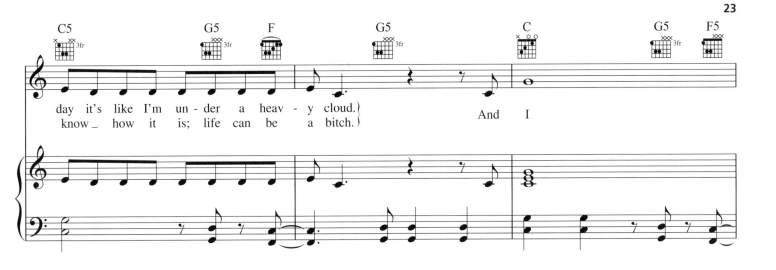

day it's like I'm un-der a heav-y cloud.
know _ how it is; life can be a bitch. And I

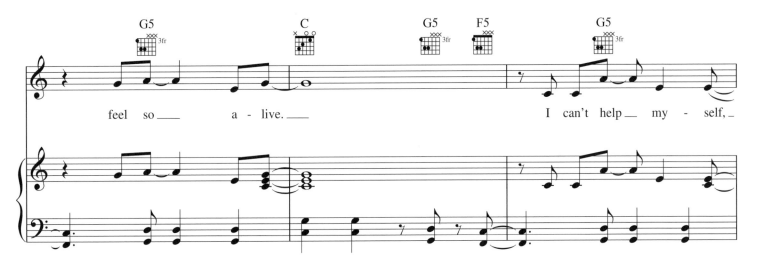

feel so ___ a - live. ___ I can't help _ my - self, _

_____ don't you re - al - ize. _____

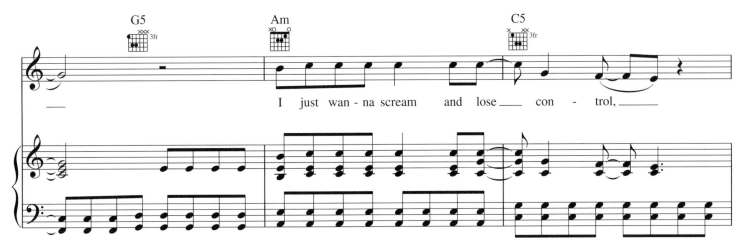

I just wan-na scream and lose ___ con - trol, _____

throw my hands up and let ___ it go, ___ for -

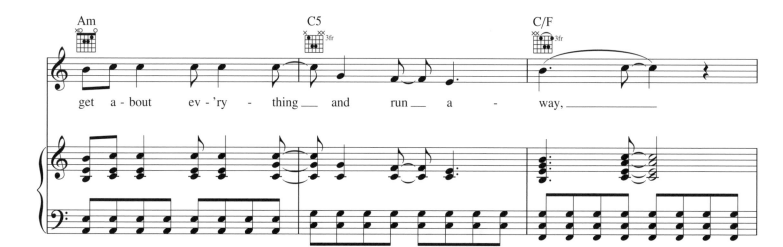

get a - bout ev - 'ry - thing ___ and run ___ a - way, ___

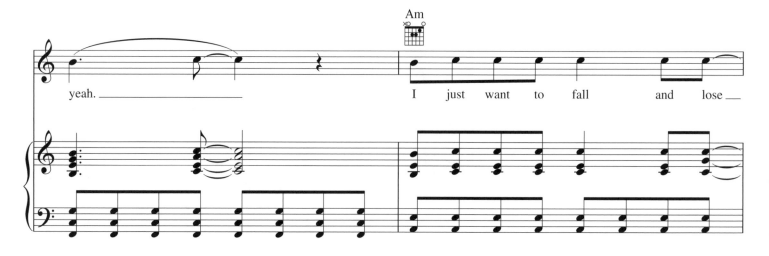

yeah. ___ I just want to fall and lose ___

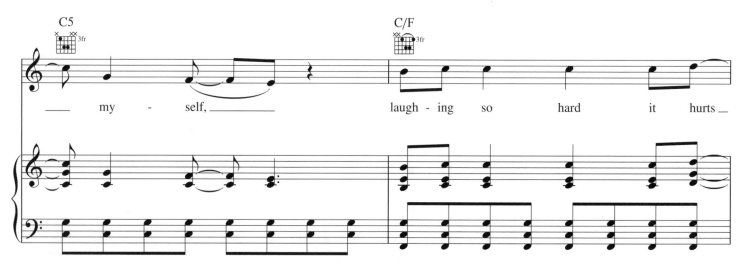

___ my - self, ___ laugh - ing so hard it hurts ___

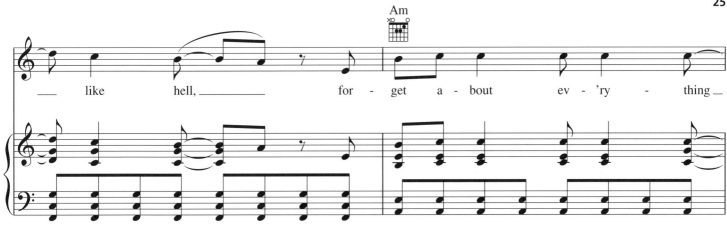

____ like hell, _____ for - get a - bout ev' - ry - thing _____

____ and run ___ a - way, _____ yeah. _____

_So - yeah. _____

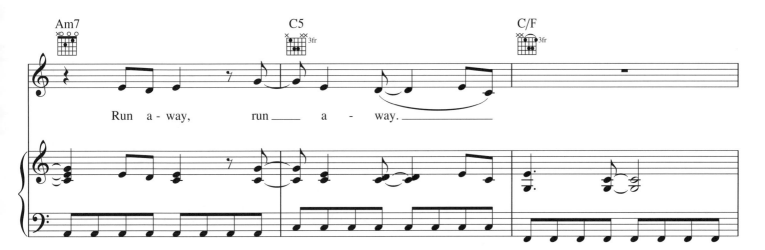

_Run a - way, run ____ a - way. _____

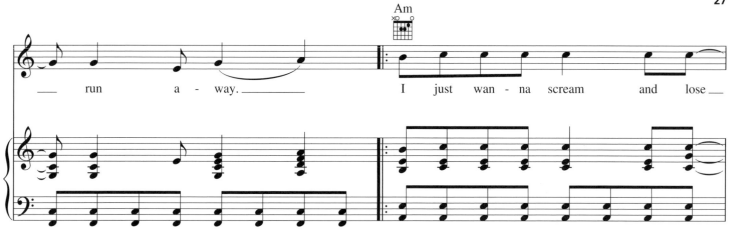

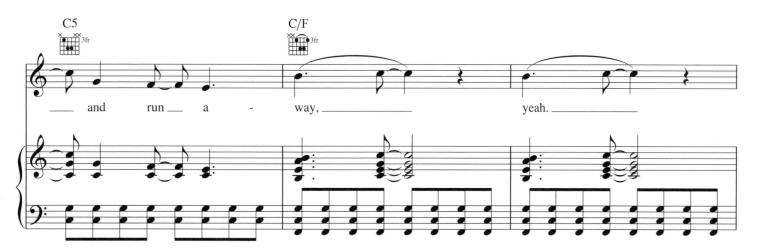

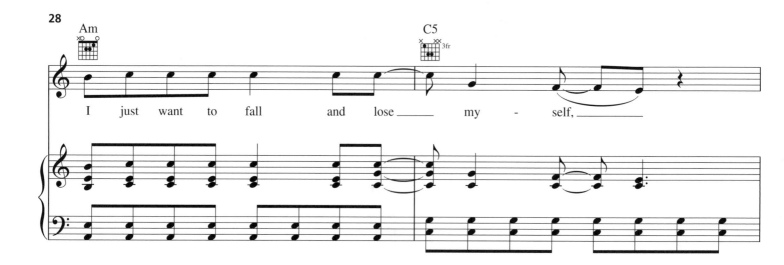

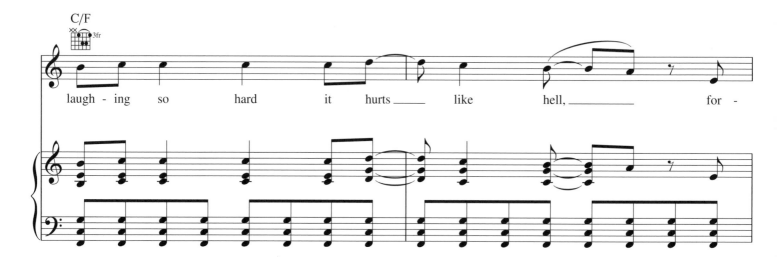

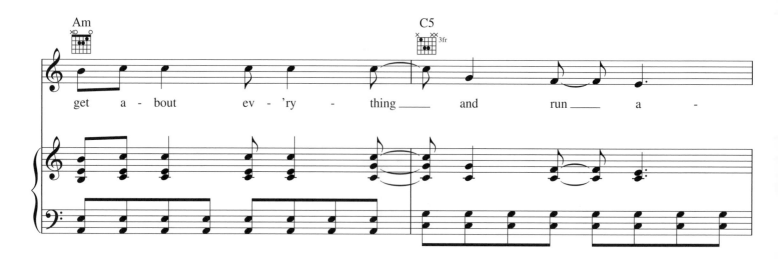

THE BEST DAMN THING

Words and Music by AVRIL LAVIGNE
and BUTCH WALKER

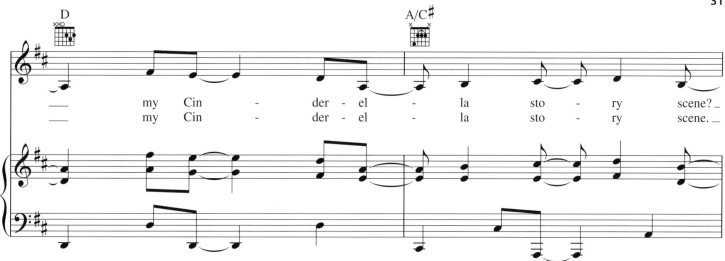

my Cin - der - el - la sto - ry scene?
my Cin - der - el - la sto - ry scene.

When do you think they'll fin - 'ly see
Now ev - 'ry - bod - y's gon - na see

that you're not, not, not gon - na get
that you're not, not, not gon - na get

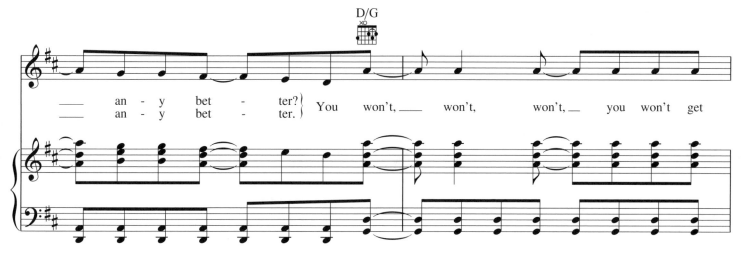

an - y bet - ter? You won't, won't, won't, you won't get
an - y bet - ter.

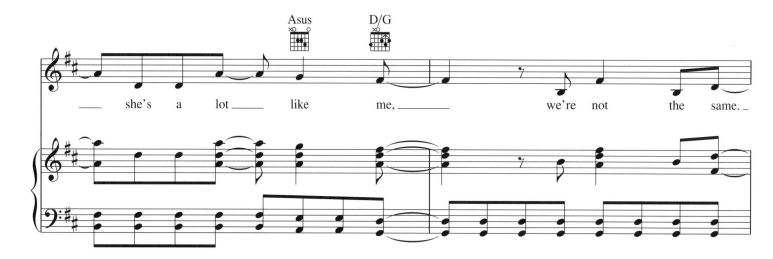

D.S. al Coda

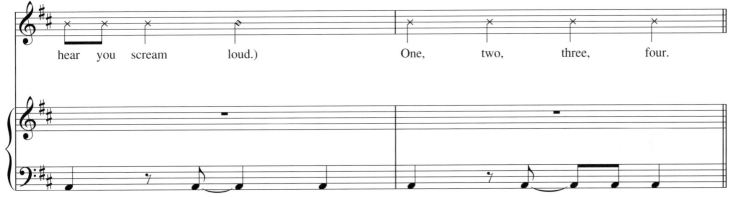

hear you scream loud.) One, two, three, four.

CODA

A5   D5

eyes have ev-er seen. Let me hear you say,

"Hey, hey, hey!" (Hey, hey, hey!) Al-right, _

now let me hear you say, "Hey, hey, ho!" (Hey, hey, ho!)

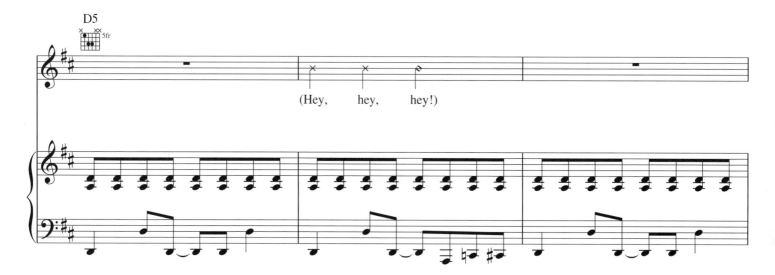

D5

(Hey, hey, hey!)

(Hey, hey, hey!) (Hey, hey, hey!) I'm the

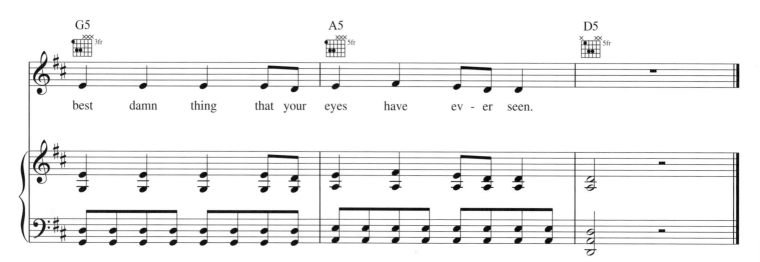

G5   A5   D5

best damn thing that your eyes have ev - er seen.

WHEN YOU'RE GONE

Words and Music by AVRIL LAVIGNE
and BUTCH WALKER

al - ways need - ed time _ on my own. _____
nev - er felt _ this _ way _ be - fore. _____

I nev - er thought I'd _____
Ev - 'ry-thing that I do _____

need you there when I _ cried. _____
re - minds me of _ you. _____

And the
And the

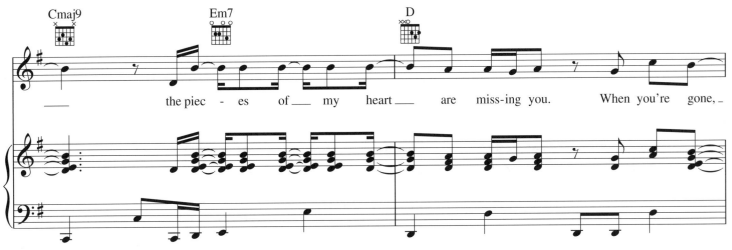

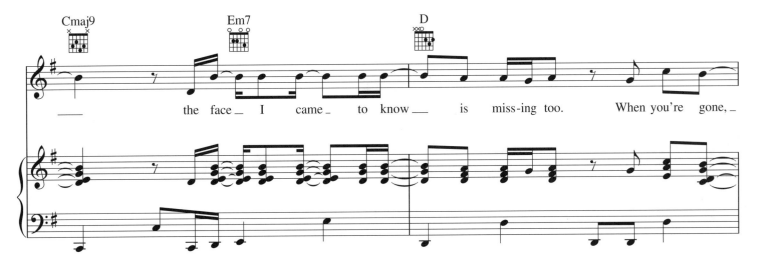

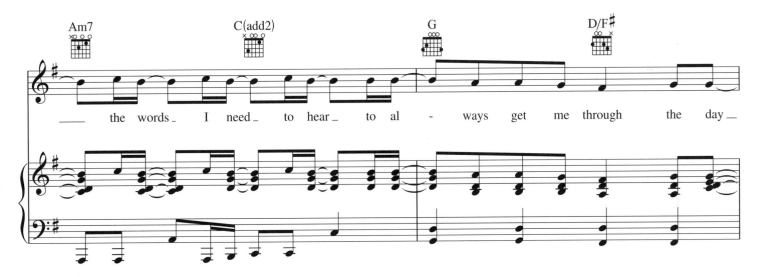

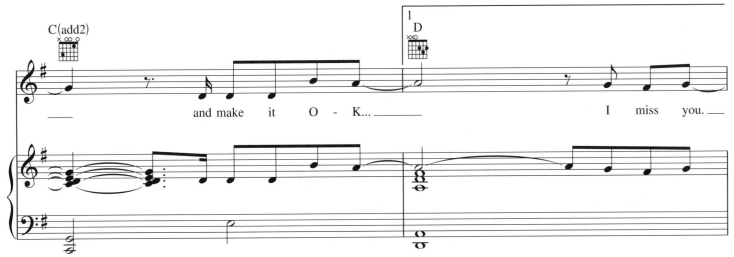

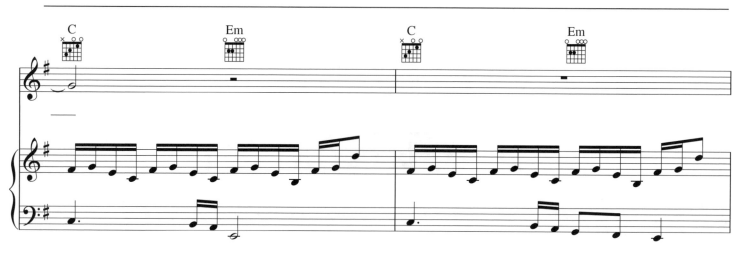

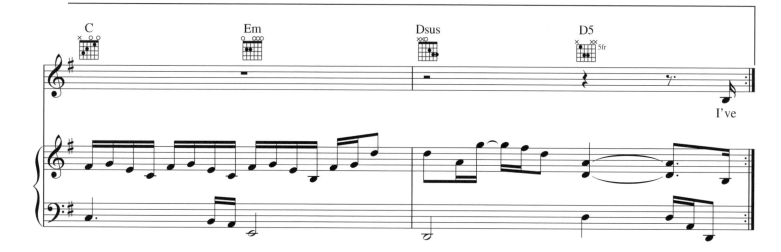

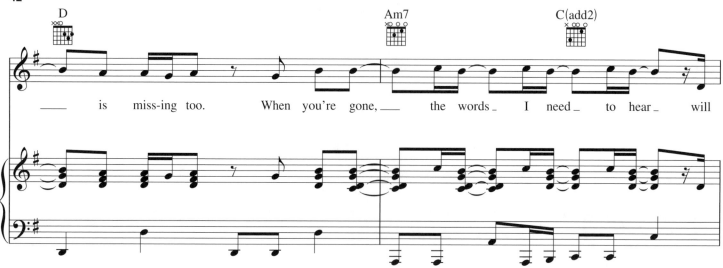

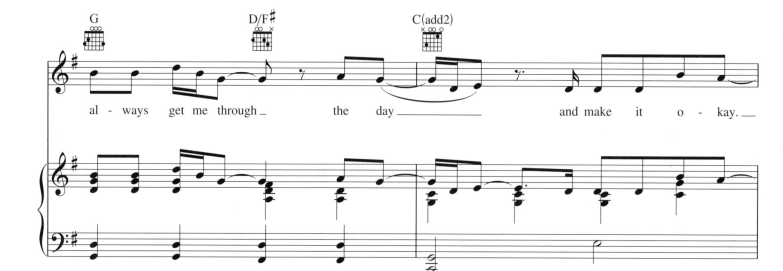

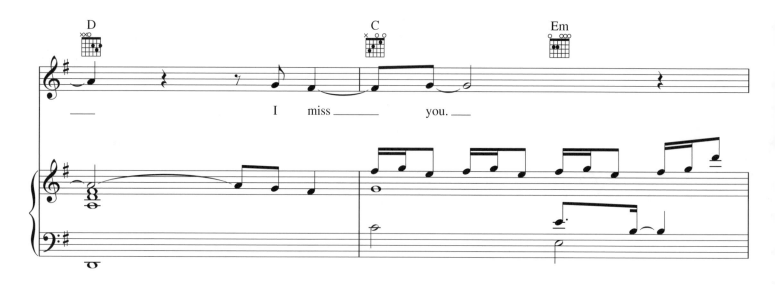

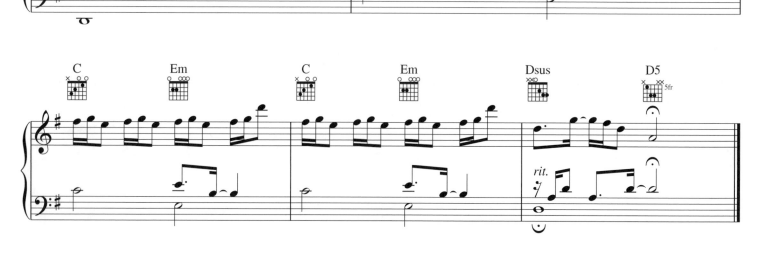

EVERYTHING BACK BUT YOU

Words and Music by AVRIL LAVIGNE
and BUTCH WALKER

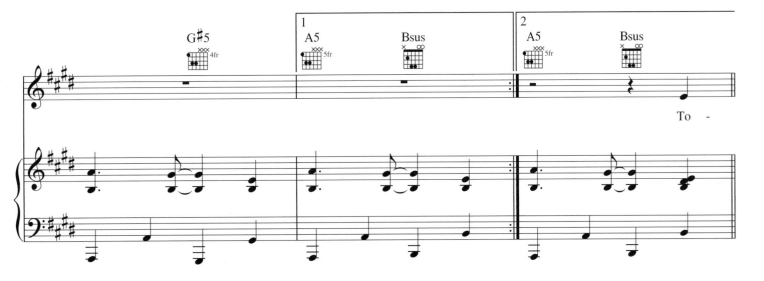

To -

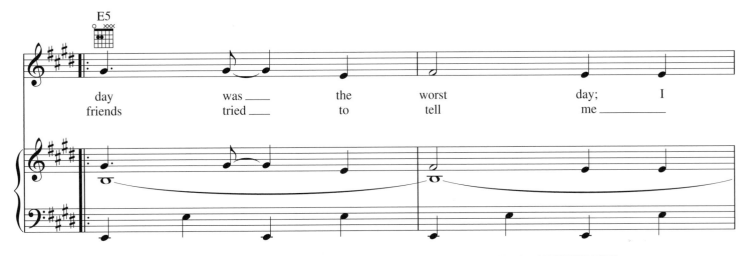

day ___ was ___ the worst day; I
friends tried ___ to tell me _____

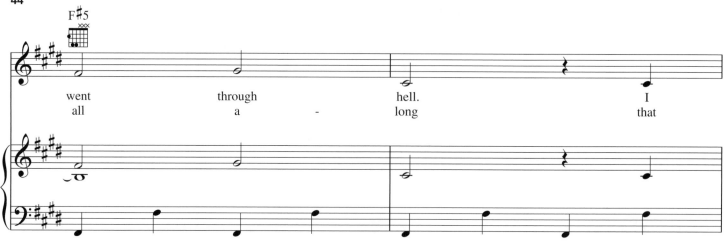

went all through a - hell. long I that

wish I could re - move it from my _____ mind.
you _____ weren't the right _____ one for _____ me.

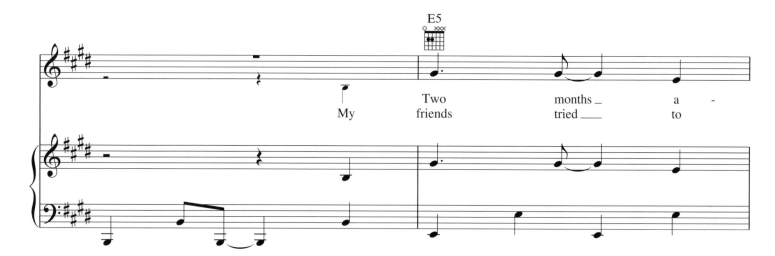

My Two friends months ___ a-

way from you, but I could - n't
tell _____ me _____ to be _____

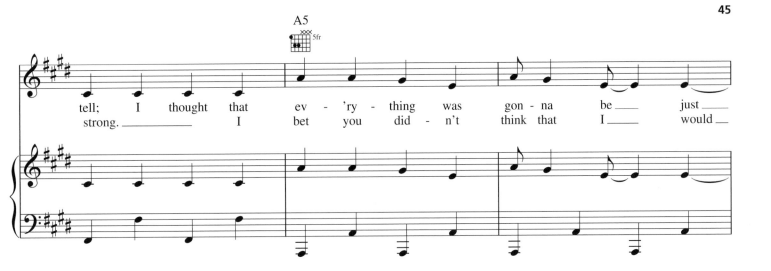

tell; I thought that ev - 'ry - thing was gon - na be ___ just ___
strong. ___ I bet you did - n't think that I ___ would ___

___ fine.
___ see.
The

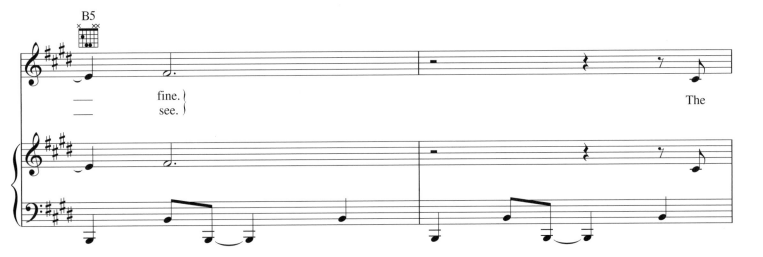

post - card that you wrote with the stu - pid lit - tle

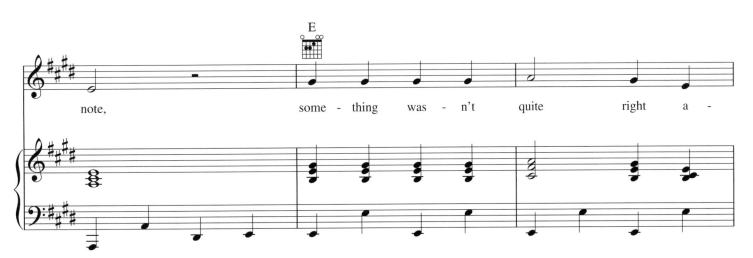

note, some - thing was - n't quite right a -

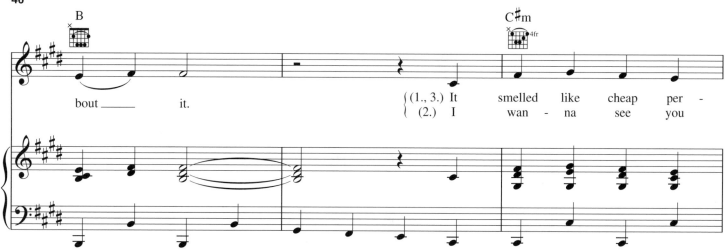

bout ____ it.
((1., 3.) It smelled like cheap per-
(2.) I wan - na see you

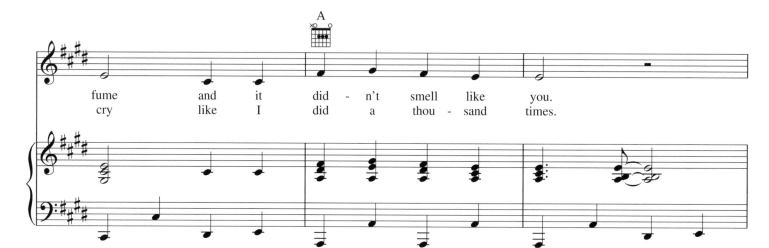

fume and it did - n't smell like you.
cry and like I did a thou - sand times.

There is no way you can get a - round ____ it, } be -
Now you're los - ing me, you're los - ing me ____ now }

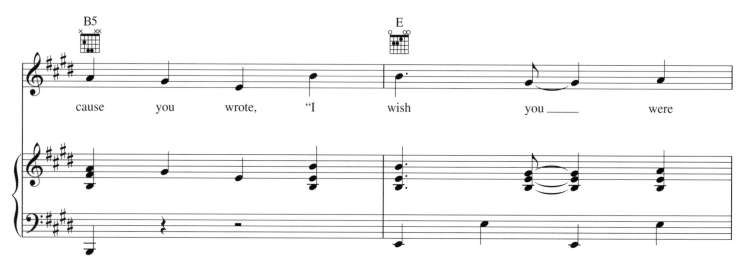

cause you wrote, "I wish you ____ were

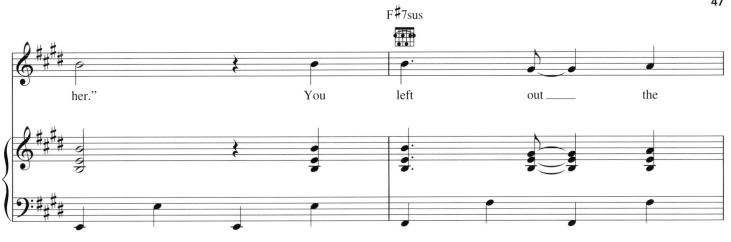

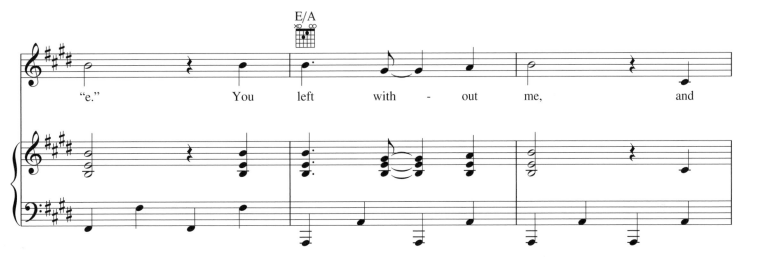

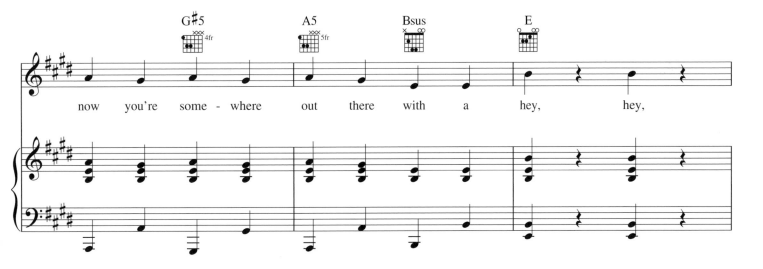

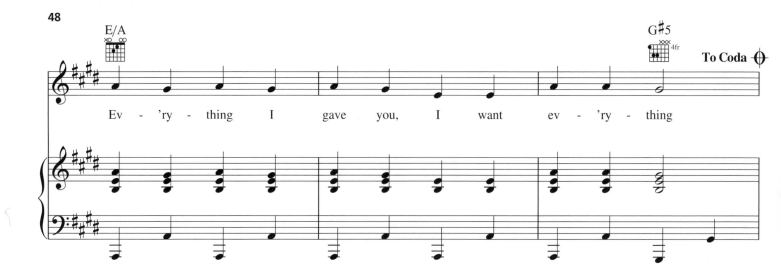

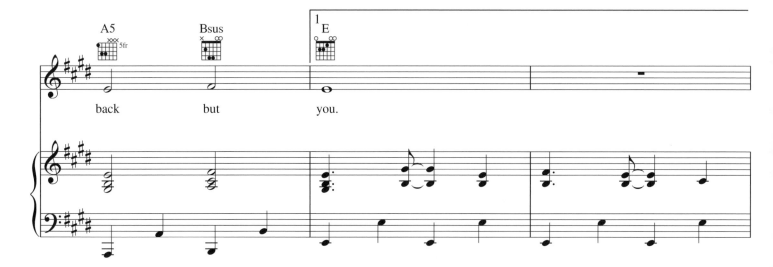

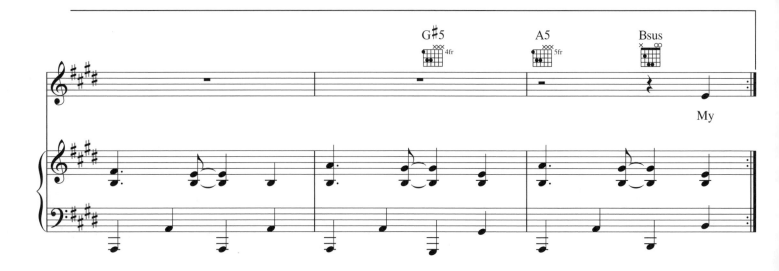

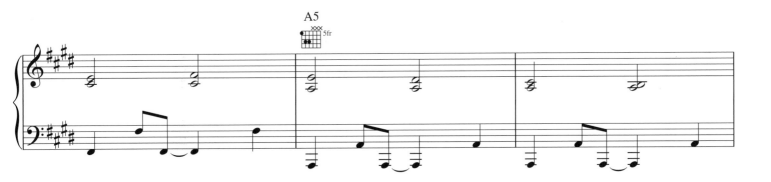

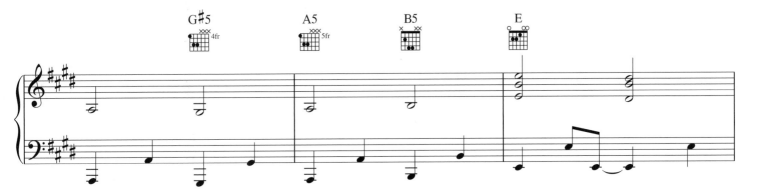

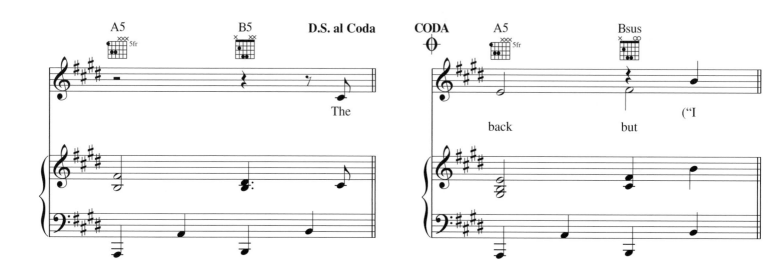

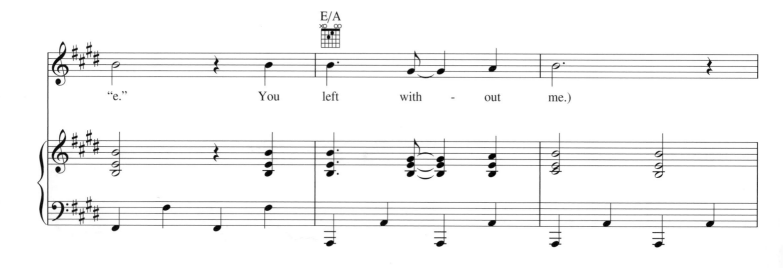

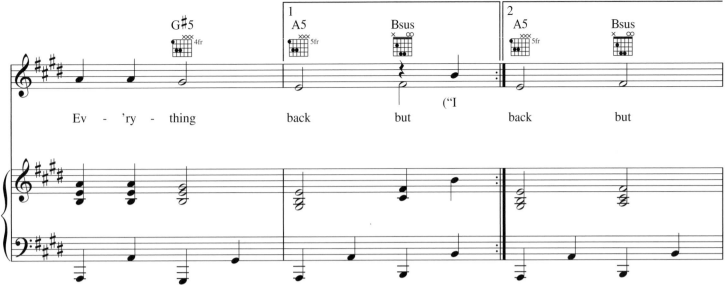

Ev - 'ry - thing back but back but ("I

you. _____

HOT

Words and Music by AVRIL LAVIGNE
and EVAN TAUBENFELD

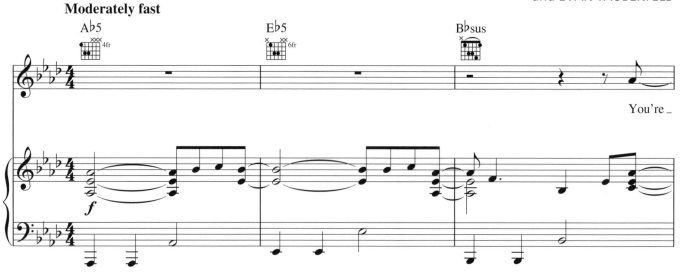

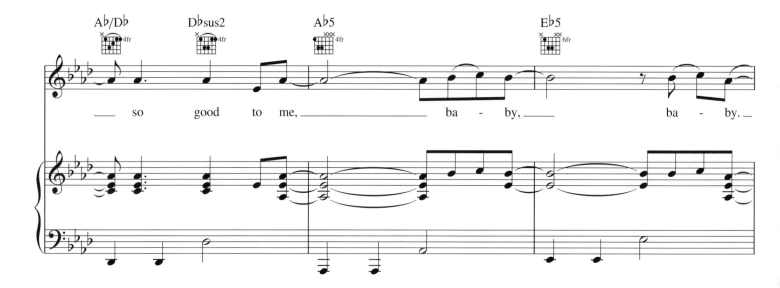

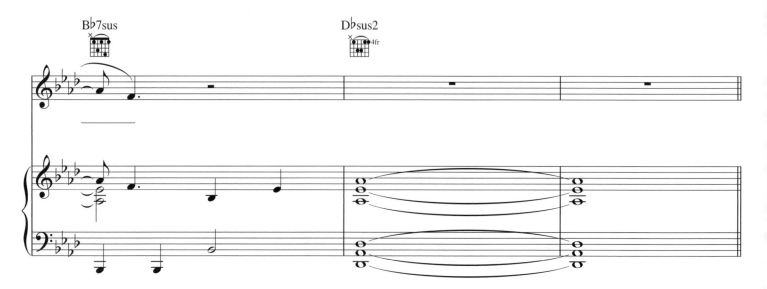

I want to lock you up in my clos-
I can make you feel ___ all bet-

-et, where no one's a-round. ___
-ter, just take it ___ in, ___

I want to
and I can

put your hand in my pock - et,
show you all ___ the plac - es

be -
you've

cause you're al - lowed. ___
nev - er ___ been. ___

I want to
And I can

drive you in-to the cor - ner and
make you say _____ ev - 'ry - thing that _____

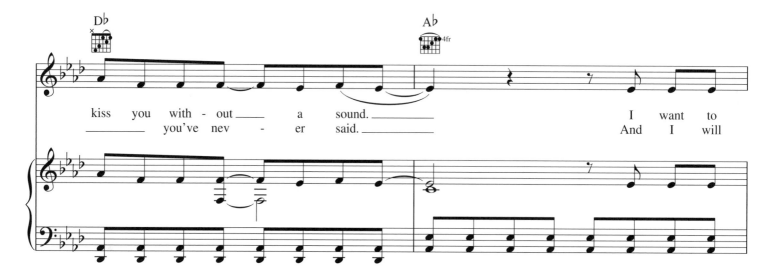

kiss you with - out _____ a sound. _____ I want to
_____ you've nev - er said. _____ And I will

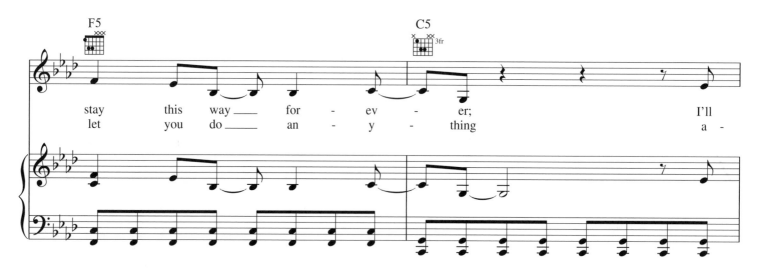

stay this way _____ for - ev - er; I'll
let you do _____ an - y - thing a -

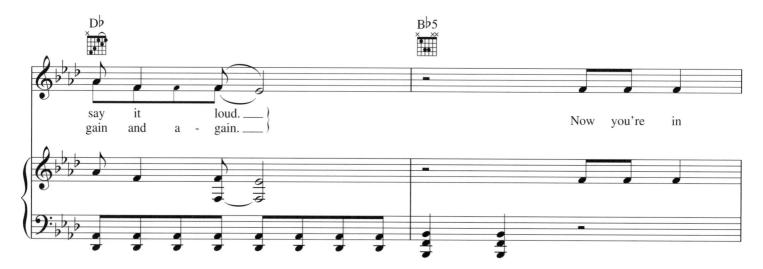

say it loud. _____ Now you're in
gain and a - gain. _____

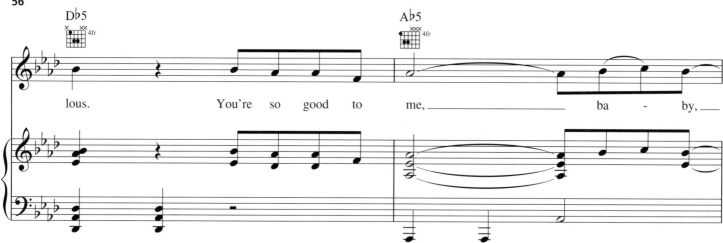

lous. You're so good to me, _____ ba - by, _____

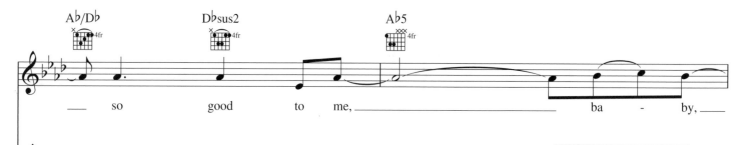

_____ ba - by. _____ You're _

_____ so good to me, _____ ba - by, _____

_____ ba - by. _____

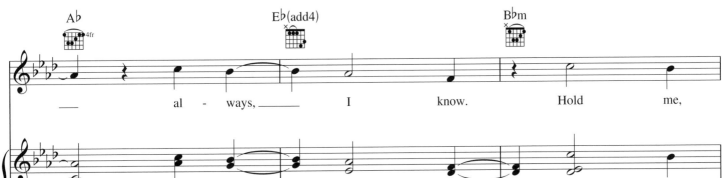

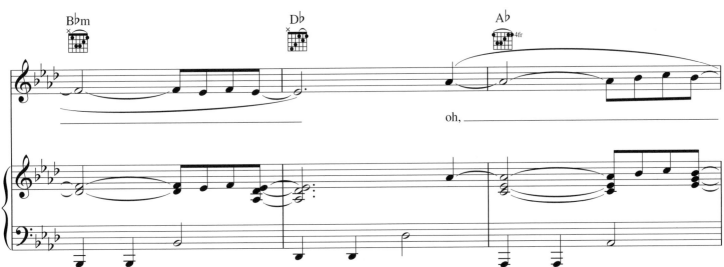

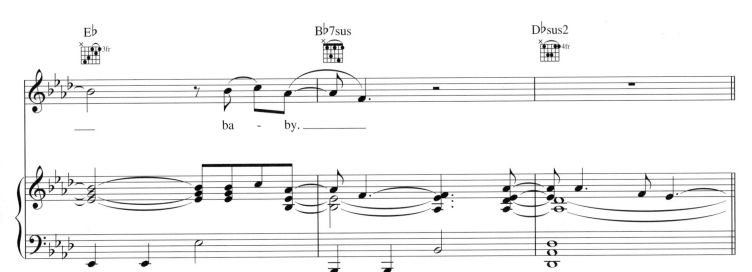

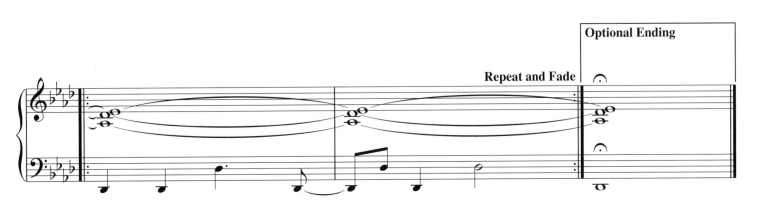

INNOCENCE

Words and Music by AVRIL LAVIGNE
and EVAN TAUBENFELD

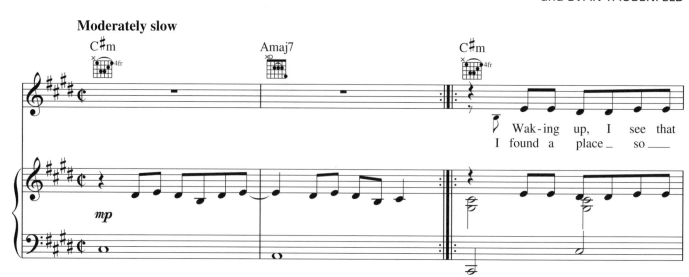

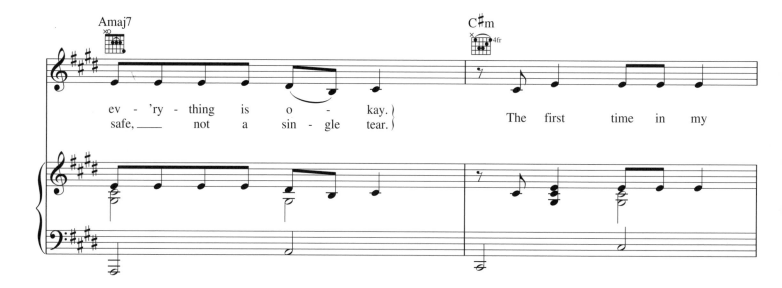

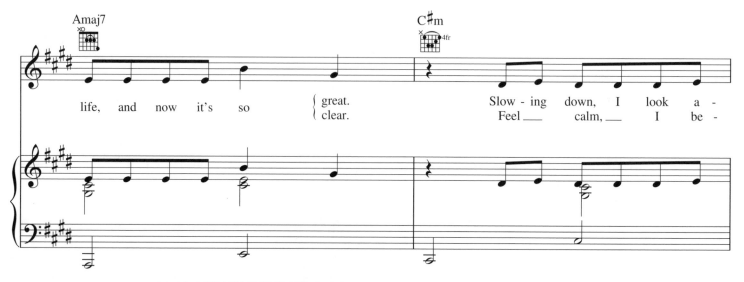

round and now I'm so a - mazed.
long, ___ I'm so hap - py here.

I think a - bout the
It's so ___ strong, and now I

lit - tle things that make ___ life great. ___
let my - self ___ be ___ sin - cere. ___

I would - n't change ___ a ___

___ thing ___ a - bout ___ it.

This is the

best feel - ing. ___

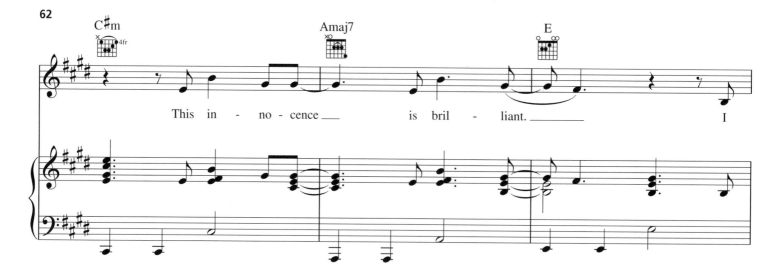

This in - no - cence ___ is bril - liant. ___ I

hope that it will stay. ___ This mo - ment is per - fect. _

___ Please don't go a - way; ___ I need _

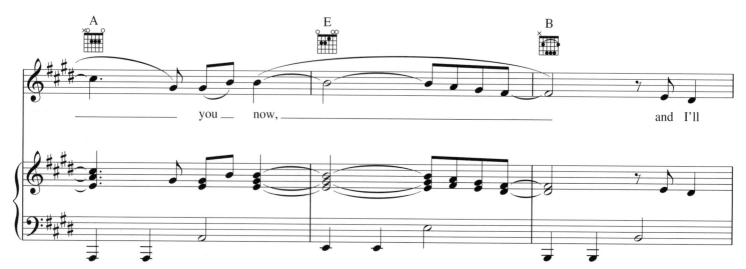

___ you now, ___ and I'll

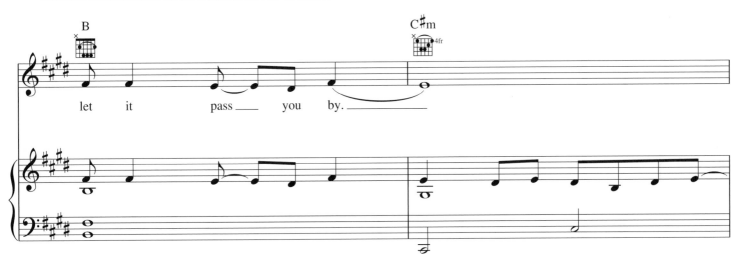

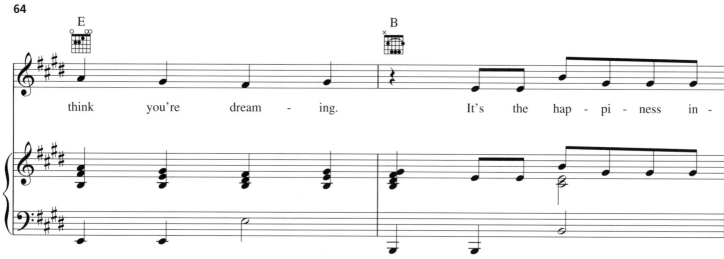

think you're dream - ing. It's the hap - pi - ness in -

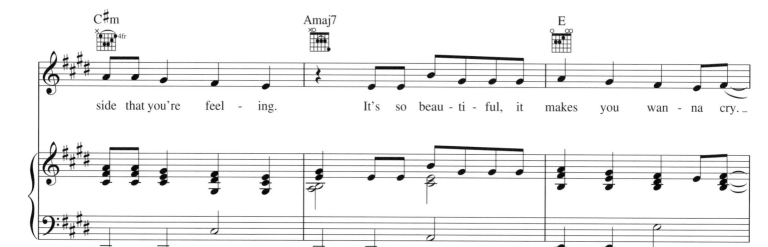

side that you're feel - ing. It's so beau - ti - ful, it makes you wan - na cry.

It's the state of bliss; you

think you're dream - ing. It's the hap - pi - ness in -

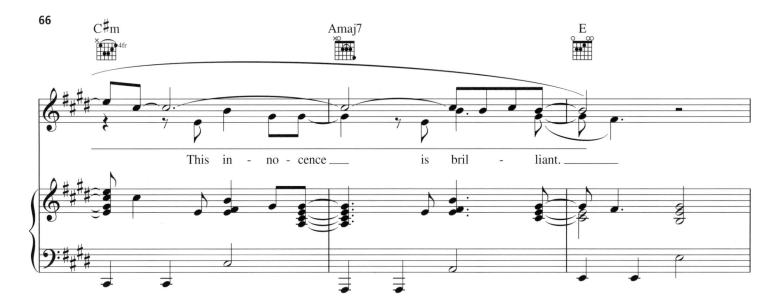

This in - no - cence ___ is bril - liant. ___

Please don't go a - way, ___ 'cause I need ___ you ___ now, ___

and I'll hold on -

to it. Don't you let it pass ___ you by. ___

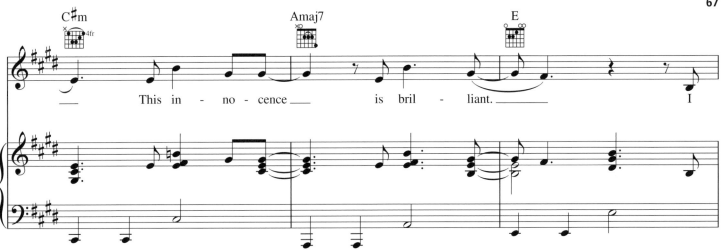

This in - no - cence ___ is bril - liant. ___ I

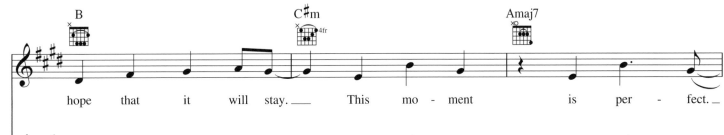

hope that it will stay. ___ This mo - ment is per - fect. ___

Please don't go a - way. ___ I need ___

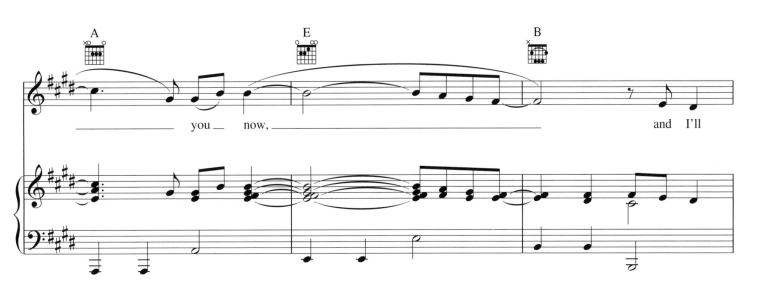

___ you ___ now, _____ and I'll

hold on - to it. Don't you

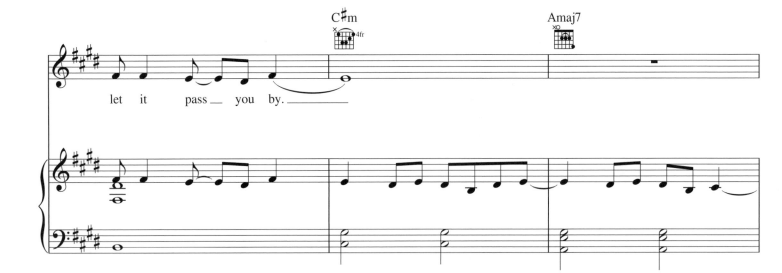

let it pass __ you by. ___

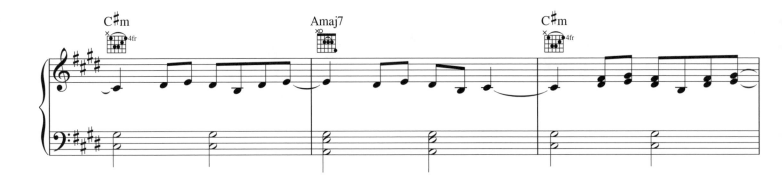

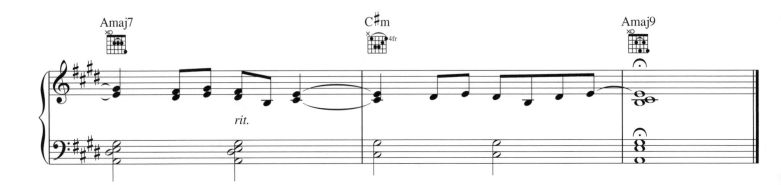

rit.

I DON'T HAVE TO TRY

Words and Music by AVRIL LAVIGNE
and LUKASZ GOTTWALD

Fast

I'm the one, I'm the one who knows ___ the dance.
I'm the one who ___ tells you what ___ to do.

I'm the one, I'm the one, who knows ___ the prance.
You're the one, you're the one, if I ___ let you.

I'm the one, I'm the one who wears ___ the pants.

Recorded a half step lower.

I wear the pants.

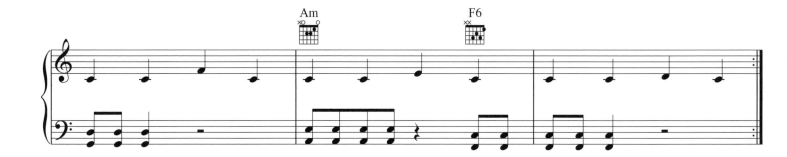

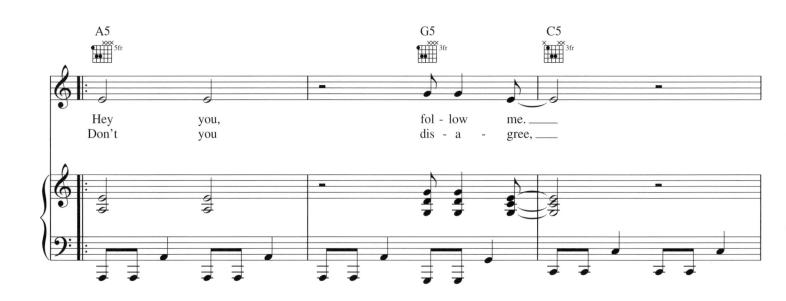

Hey you, fol - low me. _____
Don't you dis - a - gree, _____

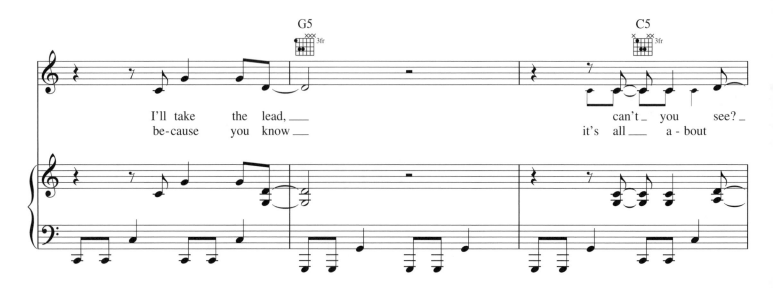

I'll take the lead, ___ can't you see? _
be - cause you know ___ it's all ___ a - bout

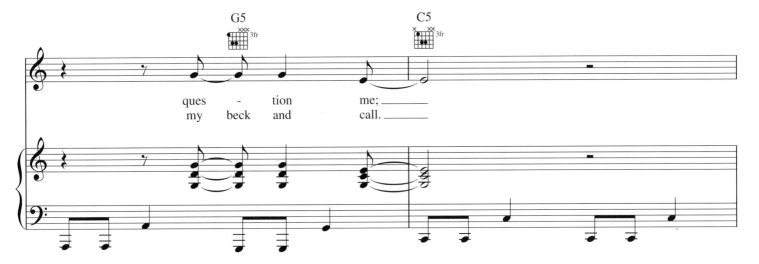

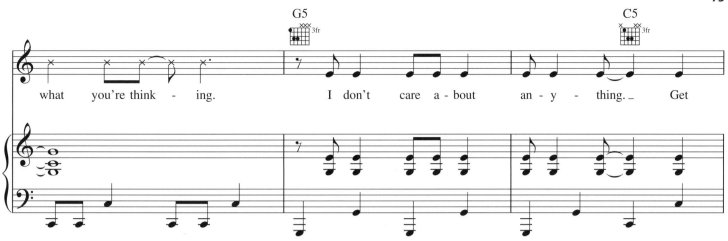

what you're think - ing. I don't care a - bout an - y - thing.__ Get

read - y, get read - y, 'cause I'm on the scene._____ I don't

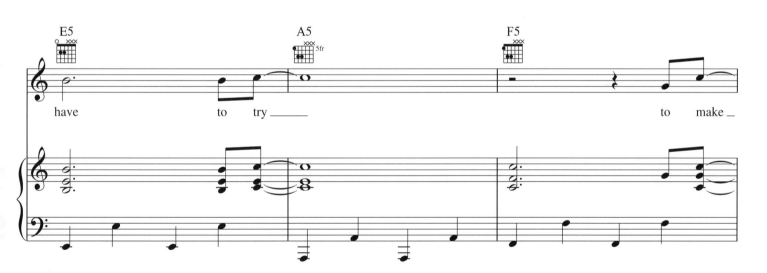

have to try ____ to make __

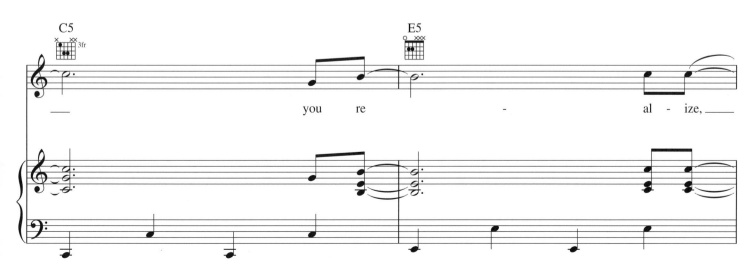

you re - al - ize, __

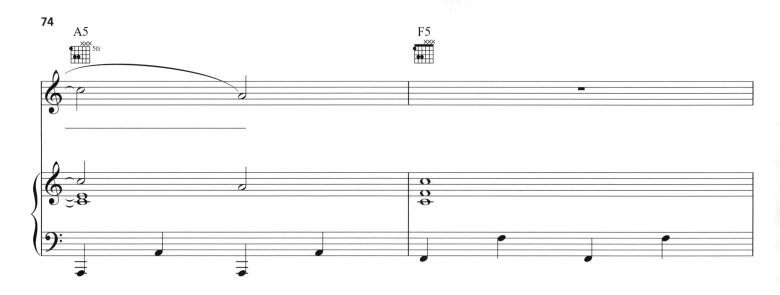

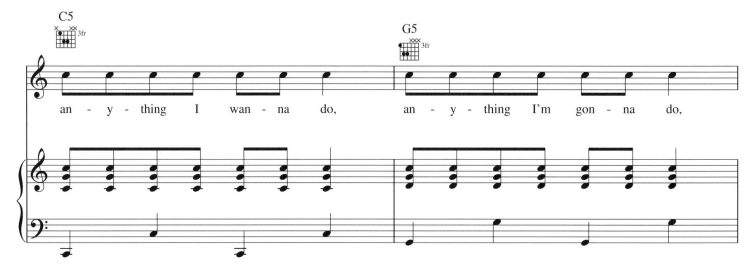

an - y - thing I wan - na do, an - y - thing I'm gon - na do,

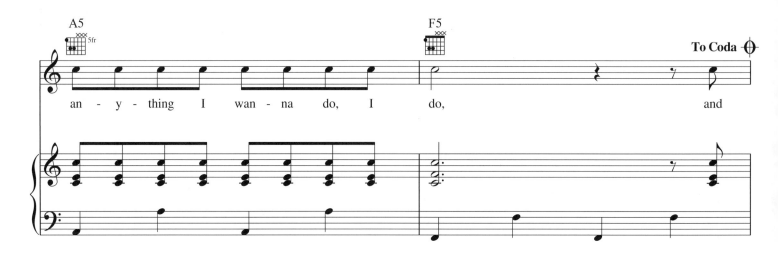

an - y - thing I wan - na do, I do, and

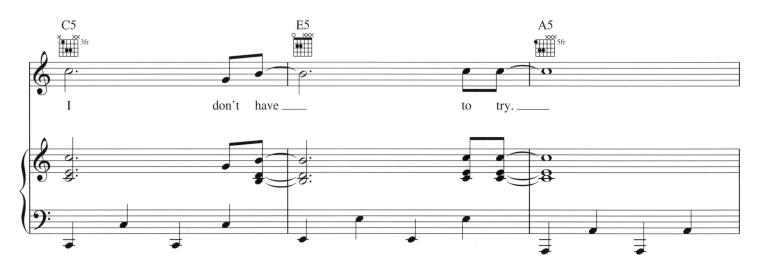

I don't have ___ to try. ___

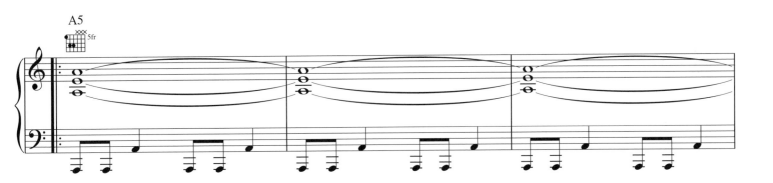

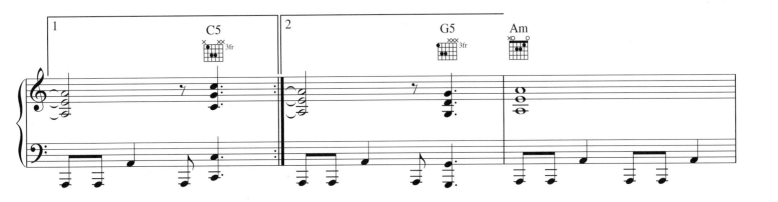

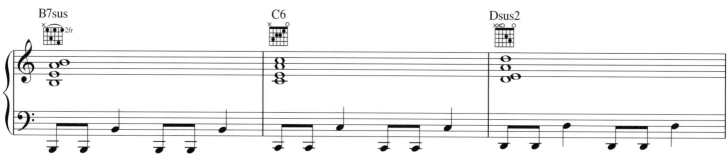

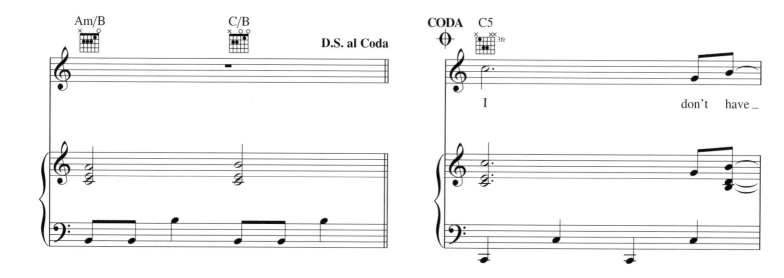

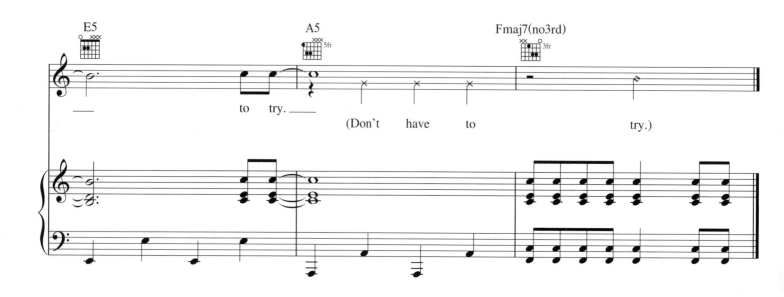

ONE OF THOSE GIRLS

Words and Music by AVRIL LAVIGNE
and EVAN TAUBENFELD

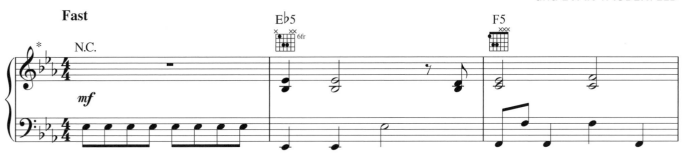

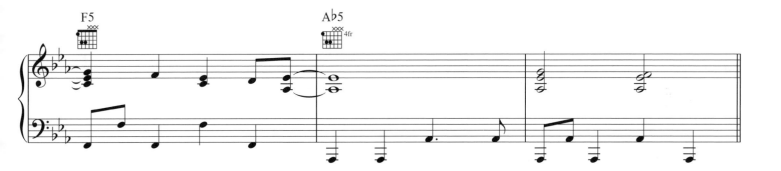

I know your _____ kind of girl. _____
She's gon - na be _____ the end of you, _____

* *Recorded one step lower.*

You on-ly care a-bout ___ one thing: ___
at least that's what ___ they say. ___

who you've seen ___ or where you've been, ___
It's been a while, ___ you're in de-ni -

- al, and now it's too late. ___
who's got mon - ey. ___

I see that look ___ in your eyes; ___
The way she looks, ___ it makes you high. ___

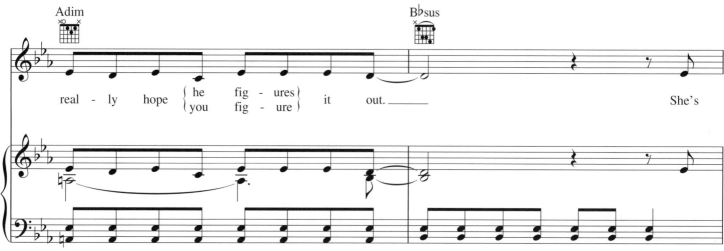

real - ly hope { he fig - ures / you fig - ure } it out. ___ She's

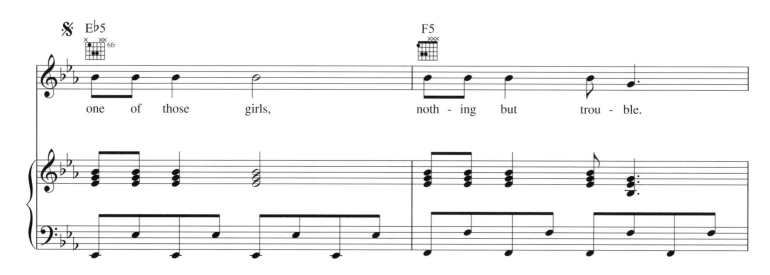

one of those girls, noth - ing but trou - ble.

Just one look and now you're see - ing dou - ble.

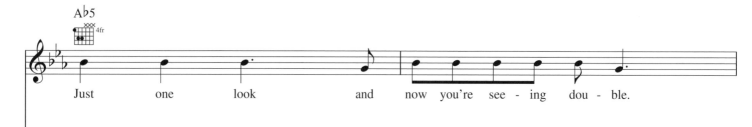

Be - fore you know ___ it she'll be gone, ___

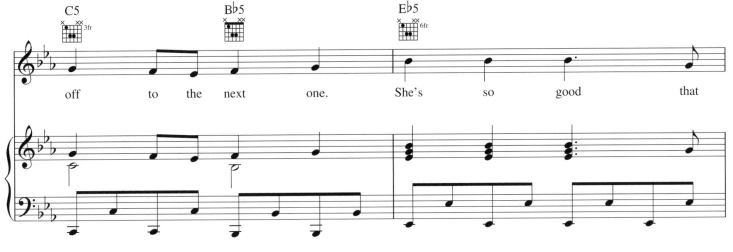

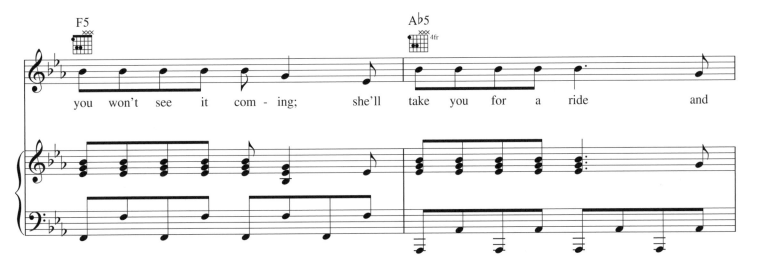

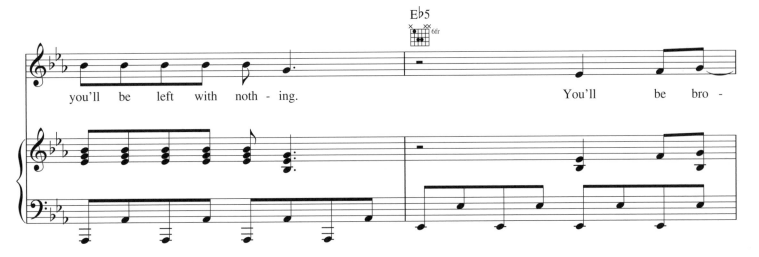

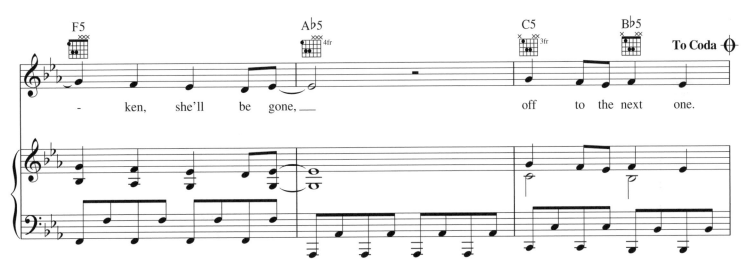

D.S. al Coda

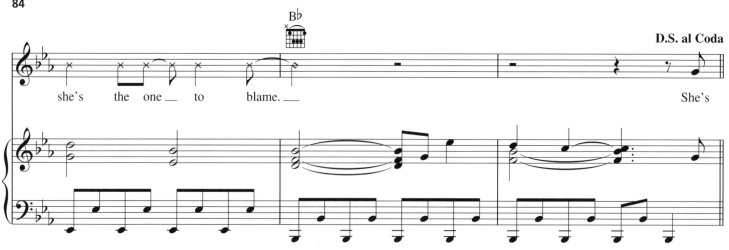

she's the one to blame. She's

CODA

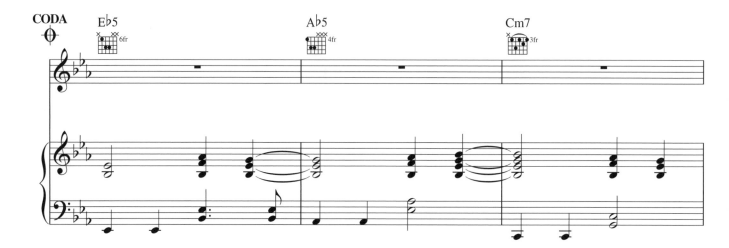

Off to the next one.

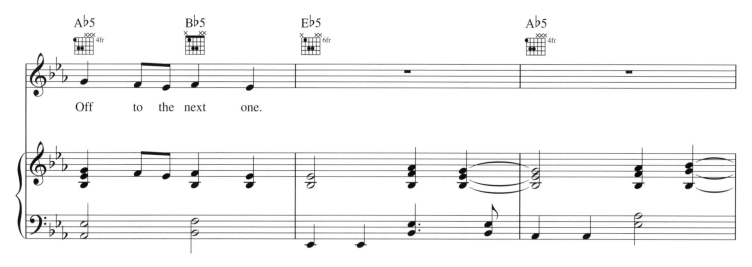

Off to the next one.

CONTAGIOUS

Words and Music by AVRIL LAVIGNE
and EVAN TAUBENFELD

Recorded a half step lower.

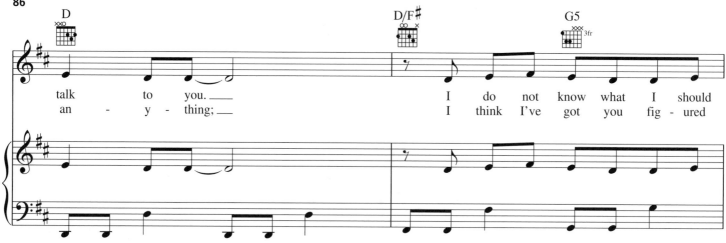

talk   to you. ____
an - y - thing; ____

I do not know what I should
I think I've got you fig - ured

say, ____   and ____ }
out.   So ____ }

I walk out ____ in si - lence. ____ That's

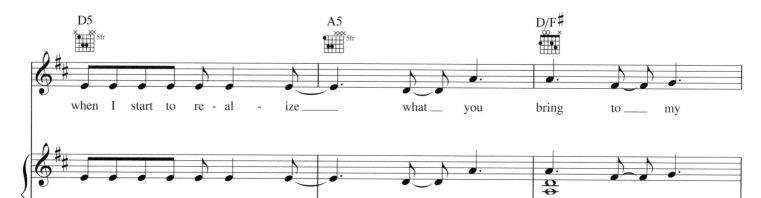

when I start to re - al - ize ____   what ____ you bring to ____ my

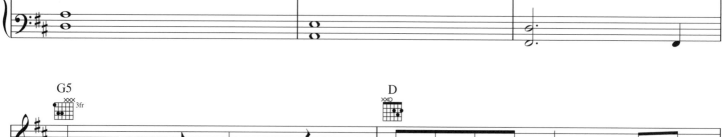

life. ____

Damn, this guy can make me { cry -
                                 { smi -

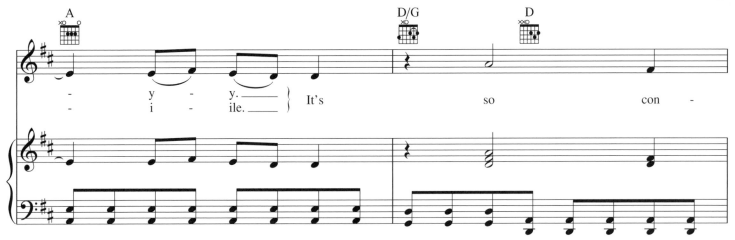

-y- y._____ } It's so con-
-i- ile._____

ta -gious.__ I can-not get____ it out____

__ of my__ mind. It's so out-ra- geous.__ You

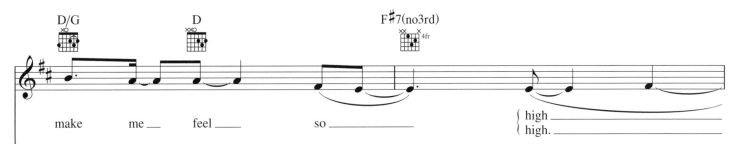

make me__ feel____ so_____ { high_____
{ high._____

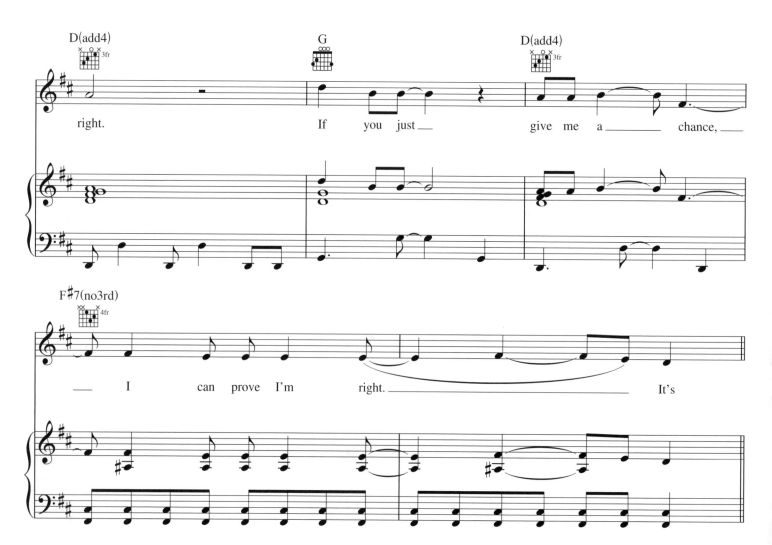

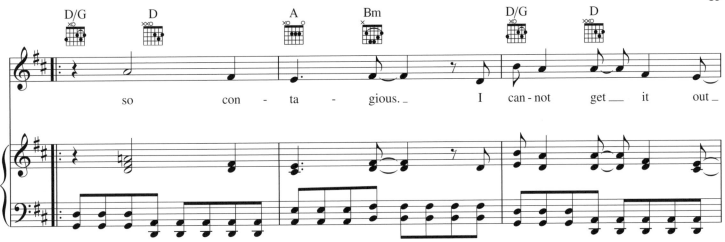

so con - ta - gious. __ I can - not get __ it out __

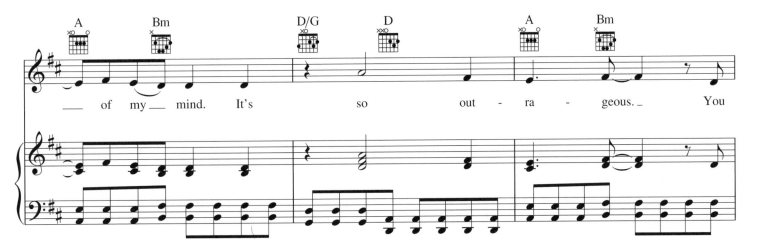

__ of my __ mind. It's so out - ra - geous. __ You

make me __ feel __ so __ high. __

__ It's __ high __ all the time. __

KEEP HOLDING ON

from the Twentieth Century Fox Motion Picture ERAGON

Words and Music by AVRIL LAVIGNE
and LUKAS GOTTWALD

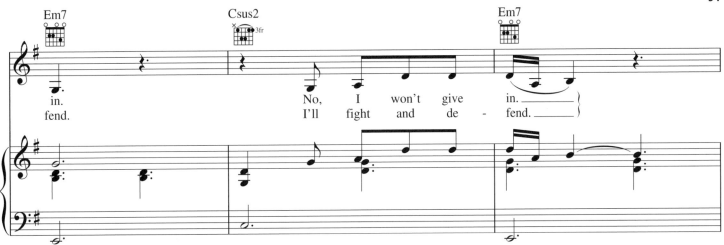

in.
fend.

No, I won't give in.
I'll fight and de - fend.

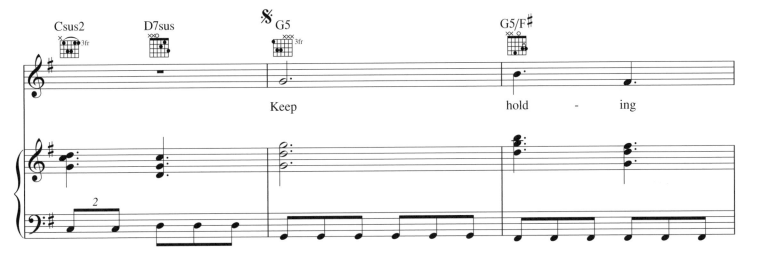

Keep hold - ing

on 'cause you know we'll make it through, we'll make it through. Just

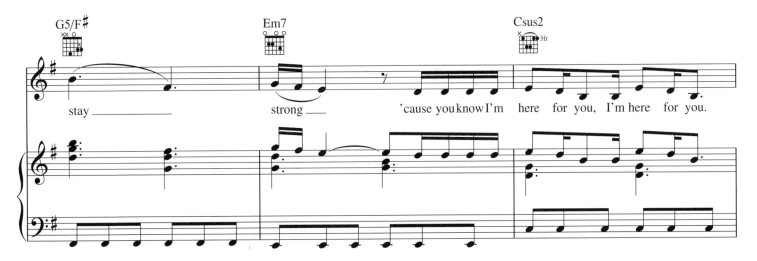

stay strong 'cause you know I'm here for you, I'm here for you.

There's noth-ing you can say, noth-ing you can do. There's no oth-er way when it comes

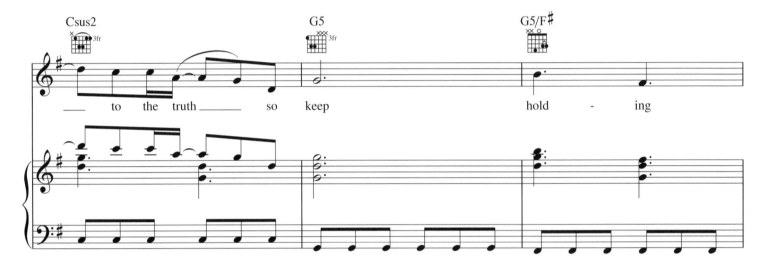

__ to the truth ___ so keep hold - ing

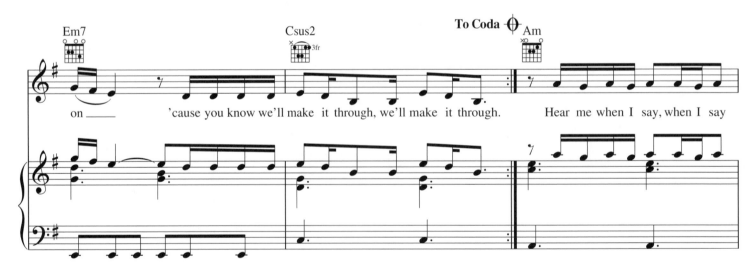

on ___ 'cause you know we'll make it through, we'll make it through. Hear me when I say, when I say

I be - lieve that noth-in's gon-na change, noth-in's gon-na change des - ti - ny. __

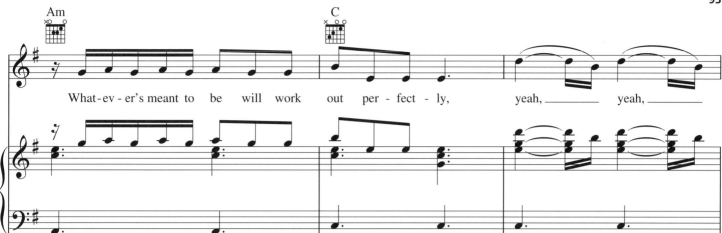

What-ev-er's meant to be will work out per-fect-ly, yeah,_____ yeah,_____

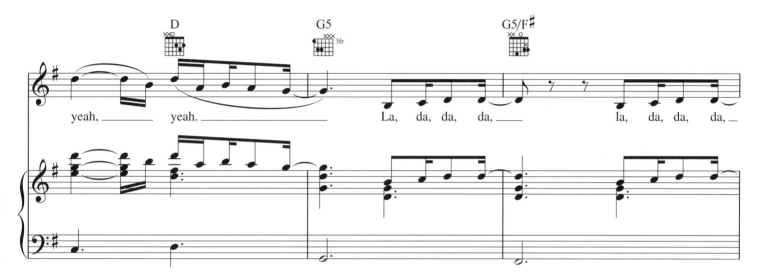

yeah,_____ yeah._____ La, da, da, da,_____ la, da, da, da,__

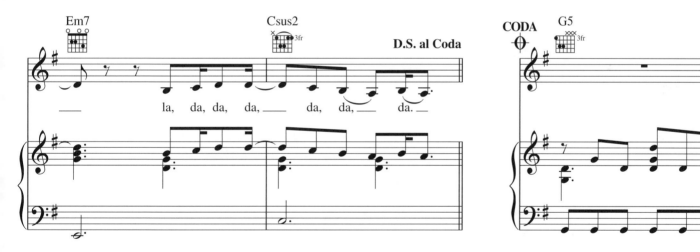

D.S. al Coda

CODA

_____ la, da, da, da,_____ da, da,_____ da.__

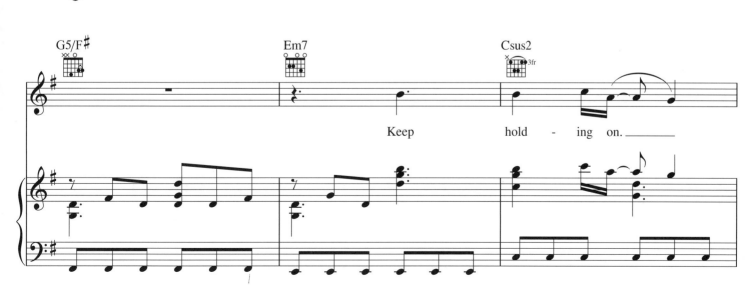

Keep hold - ing on._____

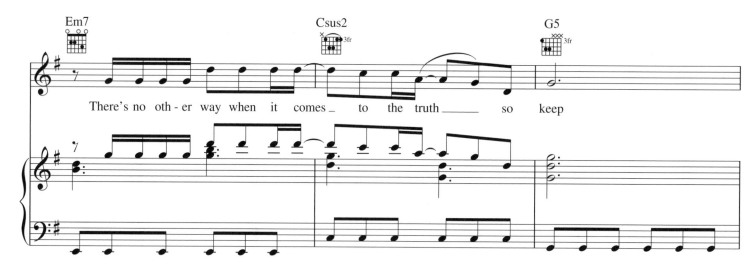